Call It What You Will © 2022 Luke Hudson

Presentation by *BookLeaf Publishing*

Web: www.bookleafpub.com

E-mail: info@bookleafpub.com

ISBN: 9789357446594

First edition 2022

Call It What You Will

Luke Hudson

BookLeaf Publishing

India | USA | UK

DEDICATION

This book is dedicated to my parents.

Mum and Dad.

The two best parents anyone could have wished for.

ACKNOWLEDGEMENT

There are many people I would like to thank
who have helped me throughout this journey but
none more so then Charlie Webb. Without you I
wouldn't be here.
Another big thank you goes to my parents Susan
and Richard Hudson. I kept this book as a
surprise to them, thank you for making me the
person I am today.

Thank you also to my proof readers' Jack
Hudson and Tyler Rooker. Two people who have
helped me through this more then they will
know.

Thank you to Jessica Lee for telling me about
this opportunity.

Also a thank you to everyone who has helped
me throughout my poetry career. To name a few:
Louie Haslam-Chance, Chris Tindall, Kathryn
Rookes, Jake Williams, Jonathan Whyatt,
Megan Spence-Hill, Bethany Brown, Katie
Brotherton, Caitlan Brewster-Craig and Beth
Renhard.

Again. Thank you.

PREFACE

This is my first book and was more a test to myself to see if I could. It took a long time to get it to be somewhere I was proud of, but I have finally got it there.
It takes a journey through my most recent writings where some are opinions on the working world and how civilization is becoming tedious and dull. Then some are fiction. It's your job to work out which.

Two Ducks

A tranquil lake,
Summer time,
Two ducks swim together,
Casting a gentle wave behind.
A ripple even.

These two ducks,
Lifelong partners,
They have a little island,
With a weeping willow,
Sheltering them when the winds high,
Shedding its leaves to build a nest.

Their quacks carry,
On such a still day,
Seemingly, forevermore.
Like the love they share,
It's endless.

Two ducks,
Maybe one day a family of ducklings too,
Little yellow balls,
On the island,
Keeping two ducks busy,
But happy.

Somewhere in the future.

For now,
Our ducks swim,
Laze together,
Love each other.

Forevermore.

I Apologise For The Things That Need No Apology. Sorry

All these things.
Trees filled with leaves,
Minds full of thoughts,
Events outside of my control,
Truly, deeply, I am sorry.

I want to howl,
I want to lose it.
I want to be a respected,
Member of society.
I need to take a hammer,
Smash this world,
Into a million fragments,
Grind them with my bare foot.

But how can we?
Locked in this cage,
Wrought iron chains,
Shackling us down even further.
How can we escape?

When our minds are held in prison,
Of our own devices,
A social prison,
One of opinions, status,
Community standing.

Howling beast inside,
Brays on this concrete floor,
Rage induced pounding,
Let me escape,
Let me free,
You officers of your own oppression.

If you break, you're weak,
If you crack, you're strange.
If you slip, you're shunned.

I feel it in my bones,
Taught chains, muscles ready to pounce,
Still the metal sits.
Waiting for an outburst,
To kill the spirit,
Before an attempt is even made.

All these things,
All these little things,
Fluttering in the mind,
In this cage,
In this world.

Let me out,
One turn of the key.
Freedom.

This world is unforgiving,
You make your own freedom,
Those without enough conviction.
Suffer incarceration endlessly.

Apologise, apologise,
Tell me again you're sorry,
Do these apologies hold forgiveness,
Or a seed of hope,
To buckle these beams of despair.

Hold a match to the sun.

I Want To Sleep But The Monkey Keeps Banging The Drum

Another story breaks,
Headlines scream to be read,
Hard hitting news all through the night.

How can you sleep?
When there is death and misery,
To film for the hungry, inhuman masses.
Twenty-four hours in a day,
And you want to waste seven sleeping.

Our thoughts and prayers,
Ever so sympathetically get extend,
To victims, their families and friends,
They get nothing more,
Then a momentary mention.
Aren't they grateful?

Propaganda,
Is how they hide their wrongs,
We demonize them,

If they spread bias,
Or call out lies.
It's our fault, when they mess up,
When they decided to air that comment.

Shut your eyes for a minute,
The world changes,
Cameras positioned somewhere else,
Nothing is ever valid,
Ever good enough,
To the big dogs upstairs.

Us, their little organ grinders,
Played like puppets for a pittance.
But we have to,
They control our jobs,
If we try speak out,
Against their regime,
Then that story gets cancelled,
We, join the line at the dole office.
They are the media,
They control.

So jump, when they say,
Fold, when they say,
We need to live don't we?

Someone else will come along,
And expose the long overdue,

Slanted truth we get.

Someone surely will,
Right?

Validate me.

Those Who Abuse, Those Who Take, And The World That Watches

My, my,
Look to the West,
What do we have here?

An unhappy sunrise,
Or a childish start to the day.
What did you expect?
Waiting for the morning,
With a scowl and a belt in hand.

Punishment doled out,
By an unjust hand,
Feels righteous to those,
Wrong accusers.

The meek servants,
Brandished by leather,
Will have revenge,

When the beds are made,
Or dinner prepared.

Those humble,
Will forgive.
Those spiteful,
Will vow vengeance.
Those in power,
Will abuse said power.

And the world,
Will keep scowling,
At its squabbling children,
Ready to buckle,
At the abuse,
Dear Mother, takes too.

A setting sun,
One day closer,
To the final straw.

Lost Mind, Lost Salvation, Lost Hope

There are two sides to every coin,
A monster lurking,
Blazing campfire, waiting, waiting.

Scattered thought,
A labyrinth of trails,
All a different tangent,
Feeding from one idea, one main,
One constant.

I wish I could say what I wanted,
Instead of getting lost in twists and turns,
A wandering mind,
Flipping a coin,
Glistening in low light,
This metal, holds value,
Little more.

Morals.

I'm not sure they exist anymore.
A fallen hero,
Toppled statue,
No hope remains.

Do you remember the established past?
I lose my way,
What came first, the blast, or the confusion?
Lithium batteries,
Remember the mundane.

We can never go back.
I suppose that's why we detour,
Keeping ourselves sane,
Our minds sustained,
With an endless stream of stimuli.

I suppose that's just one side of the argument.
There are always two.

Echoes Of Silence

Rhythm of light,
Caress these dusty pages,
As ideas pop within,
Waiting to channel outwards.

Light my page,
Warm my brow,
As I wait, for inspiration,
To shower me,
Or leave my harbour empty.

A distant gull,
Miles from shore,
Cries. For no ear will hear,
Yet its pain is no less,
Heard or not.

Satin pillows soak tears,
As well as cotton does.

No escape, but good luck.
Distant stars twinkle,
Through the dawning light,
Missed by the bustle of early morning,
Then, too late.

For the day will have taken hold,
Only night can tell its secrets.

Old aches, old pains,
Dull throbbing.
Eyes closed,
Directions on the back of a hand,
Simple remedy, swear me in,
Mother Mary,
Mother Mary.
Never ease, for I make those long ago mistakes,
Mother Mary, please.

What is as constant as day?
But night.
Two lovers, two rivals,
Always in step,
Twilight, dawn.
An embrace, another battle,
Two constants,
Like the moon and sun,
Celestial spectators.
On night, day, the passage of time,
Human race,
All of our trials and tribulations,
May seem like nothing,
In the eyes of giants.

Clouds pattern the sky,

The gull cries,
Alone in grey cold light.
No sun,
No telling if day or night.
Cries, cries, the gull cries,
For no one to hear.

Yet all, is seen.

Bureaucratic Sunshine

Grand Opening!
New city centre attraction,
It's like a brand new place.

Take a look, away from the magnifying glass,
You see the same rundown buildings.
Sketchy handshakes on street corners,
Lifeless bodies on park benches.

It's just a flower,
At a sewage plant.
A distraction to avert from the problems,
Problems that could be solved,
With the new shopping centres' budget,
With the pointless 'Modern Art' statues,
Glorified galvanized metal.

Until it's a city for the people,
How can one benefit from civil servants?
Offer degrees and scholarships,
Only not in your own city.
Ticket to ride.

Budget cuts, budget cuts,
Closures, lack of funds,
Where is the change?
Service cuts, automated,
Nothing ever improved,
Only delays or taken away completely.

Bright colours,
Thrown on sides of buildings,
Motivational posters and bright lights,
Subliminal messages?
Positivity.

Hungry children,
Filled bellies from red paint.
Homeless,
Comforted in slumber by the fountains changing
lights.

Gentrification,
Another crime of the town planner,
Another tactic.
Don't distract from the problems this time,
Just push them to another district,
With rising prices,
Encouraging chain stores, billion pound
companies,
With shiny new store fronts,

Quote on quote, safe areas.

An abandoned building?
Here's a new designer clothes store.
The local library is about to close?
Have you seen this new fast food restaurant.
Schools are overcrowded and underfunded?
Look, a new shiny.
Ooh look this way,
Look that way.

Never towards a problem,
Never towards a solution.

Taxes increase,
Fines for traffic control,
A free attraction?
Not in the eyes of the council,
Now you pay.
Asking for funds to save the swimming pool?
Ungrateful population.

They will tell us what we need,
And when.
Remember, mandatory fun.

A suggestion box that leads to the incinerator.

Celestial Future

Gaze upon the stars,
What do they tell you?
Given the position of Venus,
What does that mean for me?

I go to you, in the dead of night,
Read my palms,
Consult the crystal ball,
Most importantly,
Ask the galaxy for answers.

Comets pass,
Bringing fortune,
Stars wink, foretelling disease.
When nothing is to be seen,
Then stay inside,
Keep the lucky charms close.

Constellations talk,
To the third eye,
Lie down, look up,
See prophecies unfold from the cosmos,
Seeing the past, present and future,
Directed by the stars,

They know all.

Keep caution from the surrounding dark,
Stars, planets, constellations,
They speak, they see.
Don't lose sight.

Brew some tea,
Do the leaves back up what you saw?

Dawn is approaching,
Your future fades,
Until tomorrow,
When your future becomes a reality.

Come back again,
When we will decide,
What the celestials have dictated.

The Water Farmer

Clock strikes,
Time for work,
Those thirsty pigs,
Demanding my water,
Fill their glass,
Watch as they scuttle,
To a dark corner,
To consume.

They fight, over my water,
Alpha males all around my watering hole,
Tensions build,
And I, poor lonely I,
Need to mop,
The blood, broken glass,
My sacred water.

It's a living,
But a living I hate,
I want to keep them all away,
Have the water for myself.
Bills need to get paid,
Broken windows replaced.

The faces I see,
Regular sows,
Or new born pups.
At the end of the day,
Their money's the same,
Just some more livestock,
To keep the chains greased.

All these thoughts,
As I fill and refill,
Glass after glass,
Of my damned precious water.
It's all the same.

Same water,
Same hours,
Same animals,
Same place.

The last glass of the day I fill,
Is mine own.

The bitterest glass of all.

Current Affairs

I sense war.

I see tensions flare,
I see innocence left,
I see the power,
Turn its back. Abandonment.

I see instability,
Within and further afield.

Smoke rises,
Bombs ring out,
I open my eyes,
And I see it's no longer in my imagination,
Strap a gun to my back,
Let me fight the big mans' war,
That no one involved,
Wants to be a part of.

Can the planet handle another?
I doubt it.
But we have not learnt,
So, more fool us.
Wars for nothing,
Measuring how far you can piss.

More fool us.

I see death,
I see grey, metal,
I see grey, skies.

I sense.
War.

The Colour Of

Red for apples,
Yellow for bees,
Blue for the ocean,
And green for the summers trees.

Just like the alphabet,
Each colour has a representative,
White for the skull,
Black for the approach of death.

Innocence and exposure,
A representative for each.
Red for blood,
White for fresh linen,
Easily changed at a moment's notice,
Find the audience,
Play to them,
Then switch when the time comes,
To grab.

Purple for wizards,
Or purple for the poison,
Injected into your blood stream.
Purple focused in your mind,
As you feel yourself becoming weak,

Losing consciousness,
Fingers becoming numb,
Yet the purple in the needle,
Is as bright as ever.

Lay down,
Let me lull you to sleep,
With pictures of pleasant colours.

Orange for the sun,
Shining down upon you,
Your dirty corpse,
Or orange for the maggots,

Crawling in your gut.

The Usual

Days are the same,
Weeks, just repetition,
Months are mirror images,
Years, just a simulation.

Yet it's strange,
We count the hours down,
Until a new, familiar day.

A new element is added to the mix,
How long does it take?
For it to be forgotten,
By the next amazing invention,
That really, is just a new model,
With a new name and added flair.

But it excites us,
We get stupid over the new old,
An individual knows it's true,
The masses ignore.
Ignorant to the revolving door,
Our society is caught in.

Days are the same.
Spent in dull office routine,

Staring at screens, wishing for the weekend.

Weeks, just repetition.
Spent at home, wishing for a better life,
All the time screens surround us.

Months are mirror images.
Made up of the same days, and repeated weeks,
The fundamentals change, but overall?

Years, just a simulation.
That's how it feels,
Living the same day, week, month.
Over, add infinity.

So why the long face?
Pull me the same pint,
And I'll tell you,
Like I did last week,

And how I will be,
Months from now.

Down The Dump

Old refrigerators,
Burnt out cars,
Rats eating Kentucky Fried Chicken,
A baby dolls head.

What treasure to be found,
On ole Stigs' stomping ground.

Rusted bed springs,
Shattered wedding rings,
Too many unsolicited flings.

Down the dump we go,
Like Dopey and Doc,
To the mine.
Diamonds are the goal,
But too many times,
We settle for coal.

They sneer,
They smear,
When we go down the dump,
The scholars and teachers,
Government officials and preachers,
Even the milkman jeers.

My paradise, isn't in books,
Or high profile taxes,
It's in the broken junk,
Washing machines and jammed faxes.

Let them laugh,
My stained hands,
Look odd on the sterile papers,
Pristine desks,
Who wished for this life?

Down the dump,
'Fore the sun sets,
Fathers before me,
Fathers after.
We navigate the piles,
Not asking for wages from anyone.

Simple life takes its toll,
My back is hunched,
Hands of callous,
Chipped teeth,
Bent fingers.

They see a tramp,
Down the dump.

I see from different eyes,

Down the dump,
Tin cans, paint cans, sardine cans,
On the inside it holds different,
Yet outside?

Look to me.
What do you see?
Look to you,
Ask me too?

It's not so different,
Your life and home,
To mine.
Those discarded condoms,
End.
Down the dump.

Fallen Minds

Let me fall.
From arms tangled in love,
Through purgatory and limbo,
Constantly between the two,
Let me fall,
From you, until infinity.

I pass memories,
Fragmented.
Piece together as you fall,
Slate skies animated by movement,
These shared moments.
Are they good, are they bad,
What is the message?
Of why they're shown.

Let me fall.
From memory of all,
Slowly forgotten,
Until I too become one with time itself.

Stay together, yet disintegrate,
As mind and matter,
Decay into the void,
Let me surround the next sullen faller,

Until our matter merges,
To converge on yet another.

It's a process,
So let me fall.

Farther, further down,
Never landing,
Never stopping.

Becoming one with the fall.

Let me go.

What A Year

My Birthday Present died.
It wilted overnight,
Dropped its leaves,
Keeled over and simply died.

My Christmas meal left.
Packed its bags,
Gathered the sprouts,
And caught the first plane to sunny pasture.

My Valentines' card sued me.
Took my romantic poem,
Filled in a restraining order,
Damages need to be paid by next week.

My Easter egg went insane.
Shared in graphic detail,
About the Easter Bunnies' insides,
Now it's rocking back and forth, presumably
crying.

My Halloween costume declared independence.
Now my costume wears me,
It's a legal citizen now,
Has free will to do as it pleases.

My April fool's day prank told me to grow up.
It lectured me on how to be a proper adult,
How I waste my time,
And how I can be a model citizen, like it is.

My St Patricks' Day pint, drunk itself.
It now attends AA,
I'm its sponsor,
But I get told I lead it astray.

My New Years' resolution gave up on me.
It told me I hadn't any will power,
To see it through,
Left me to keep bad habits.

Well, there's always next year I suppose.

Candyman

One, two,
Bees buzzing by you.
Three, four,
There's a hook in your door.
Seven, eight,
It's getting late.

Candyman.

Ring a ring o' roses,
Candle burning in the mirror,
He loves me,
Candyman,
He loves me not.

Five times,
Said in the dark,
In the mirror,
Running water,
Boo.

Twinkle twinkle little star,
Humpty Dumpty sat on a wall,
Candyman.

Humpty Dumpty had a great fall,
How I wonder what you are.

A sailor went to sea,
A sailor went to sea,
Hail Mary, full of grace.

Candy.

Houston

S.O.S

Save Our fucking Souls.
Extend your hand to me,
Your cruel, gnarled hand,
Pull me from this plight.

Mayday, mayday, abort.
Houston,
Houston where are you?
We have a problem.

Radio silence,
Oh, Houston,
S.O.S.

I wouldn't normally,
But I beg,
My tender eyes,
Cannot contain the atrocities,
Dear Houston,
Save my god forsaken soul.

S.O.S
Dot, dot, dot,

Dash, dash, dash,
Dot, dot, dot.

I hear the bludgeon,
On my skull,
Yet I feel no pain.

Houston?

Stranger

I call to myself,
Yet I receive no answer.
I do not understand,
For I hear the call,
I articulate a response,
Only for an echo to take its place.

I look at myself,
Yet I see no body.
I do not understand,
For I stand in full view,
I move to be seen.
Only for the viewer to move on, disappointed.

I touch myself,
Yet I feel nothing.
I do not understand,
For I grasp, skin to skin,
I clutch harder.
Only to feel nothing, neither skin nor skin.

I think to myself,
Yet I have no train of thought.
I do not understand,
For I know the thought,

I try to engage the process.
Only to lose hours in an empty state.

I call,
I look,
I touch,
I think.

Nothing.

Dear

Oh fading moon,
Hide my sorrow,
Till cruel tomorrow.

Take my plight, from me now,
Until the shadows grow tall and long,
Radio playing that hurtful song.

My woe, you ask, my woe,
Who is to know?
Least of all myself.

My woe, stems,
From the existence of man,
In everything we can,
Or cannot fathom.

Death, taxes, beyond.
To name a few,
What do these things do,
To the likes of you?

Nomad

Nomad travels,
Far across the land.
Living but leaving no trace,
Like the wind,
One moment there, next not a sign.

Nomad ventures,
Only taking enough to survive,
Giving back, planting, tending,
Healing.
Lost to modernisation,
Or shunned by ignorance.

Nomad cries.
Pushed out of civilisation,
No papers, no identity.
No money, turn around at the city limits,
These cold creatures,
That share the same name,
The Human Race.
You live separate.

Nomad follows,
The sun and season,
Confused by the concrete jungles,

Tarmac rivers.
Nomad, Nomad,
Lives a simple life,
Happy with nature,
Not belittled with interest rates and taxes.

Nomad.
What is the time?

Spring time.

Moments

Moments.
That's all life is made of.
Moments.

Some are good,
Unfortunately some are bad,
But, in those moments,
It's who you're with that matters,
The friends and family,
You want to share it with.

Nothing will stop these moments from
happening,
Life will not do that for you,
Times can be made easier, however,
With kindness,
People who want to see you thrive.

Life.
Can find a way,
Of getting in the way.
Just don't forget,
Those who make life,
A little less of a challenge.

Remember those people,
Make all the moments you can, with them.
Because then,
Life.

Well, you tell me.